How Fast Is It?

A Book about Adverbs

amicus readers 3

by Cari Meister
illustrated by Holli Conger

Say Hello to Amicus Readers.

You'll find our helpful dog, Amicus, chasing a ball—to let you know the reading level of a book.

1

Learn to Read

High frequency words and close photo-text matches introduce familiar topics and provide support for brand new readers.

2

Read Independently

Some repetition is mixed with varied sentence structures and a select amount of new vocabulary words are introduced with text and photo support.

3

Read to Know More

Interesting facts and engaging art and photos give fluent readers fun books both for reading practice and to learn about new topics.

Amicus Readers are published by Amicus
P.O. Box 1329, Mankato, MN 56002
www.amicuspublishing.us

Illustrations by Holli Conger
Editor Wendy Dieker
Designer Heather Dreisbach

Printed in the United States of America.

10 9 8 7 6 5 4 3 2 1

Library of Congress Cataloging-in-Publication Data
Names: Meister, Cari, author. | Conger, Holli, illustrator.
Title: How fast is it? : a book about adverbs / by Cari Meister ; illustrated by Holli Conger.
Description: Mankato, Minnesota : Amicus, [2017] | Series: Say what? Parts of Speech. Audience: K to Grade 3_
Identifiers: LCCN 2015041493 (print) | LCCN 2015046774 (ebook) |SBN 9781607539315 (library binding) | ISBN 9781681510552 (eBook)
Subjects: LCSH: English language--Adverb--Juvenile literature. | English language--Grammar--Juvenile literature.
Classification: LCC PE1325 .M44 2017 (print) | LCC PE1325 (ebook) | DDC 428.2/4--dc23
LC record available at http://lccn.loc.gov/2015041493

An adverb is a word that describes a verb. A verb is an action word. The purple words in the story are adverbs.

Nora, William, and Arjun are at the beach. Arjun is waiting eagerly.

A boat appears nearby.
Arjun quickly jumps up.

He says, "My dad brought the boat today!"

Nora and Arjun bravely get in the boat. William nervously climbs in.

“I want to go fast!” says Nora. “How fast does it go?”

Arjun smiles wildly. “Very fast!”

“I like to go slow,” William says quietly.

“Hold on tightly,” says Mr. Parmar. At first, the boat goes slow. William smiles weakly.

Mr. Parmar gently pushes the throttle. The boat goes faster.

Nora puts her thumb up.
Mr. Parmar pushes the throttle harder.

Now the boat zooms!
It zooms here. It zooms there.

“Whee!” yells Nora. She waves happily at Arjun.

Waves splash roughly into the boat. William looks horribly sick.

Mr. Parmar quickly stops the boat.

“Sorry, William,” he says. “I see you don’t like to go fast.”

"I have an idea," says Arjun. He pulls out a little boat. He quickly blows it up.

Now everyone is happy.
William's boat goes slow.
Their boat goes fast!

Jobs of an Adverb

Adverbs tell us how something happens.

Waves splash roughly into the boat.

Adverbs tell us where something happens.

A boat appears nearby.

Adverbs tell us when something happens.

My dad brought the boat today!